About this

This book is intended to give you a snapshot
of our beautiful Island - both in terms of its beauty
and a brief introduction to some of the wonderful
and diverse produce we have available here,
via recipes and photos of the island.

The recipes cover traditional dishes, passed down
in families over the years and also, some of the
products that have enjoyed popularity in more recent
times, with a brief history of the town markets, the
tomato industry and the celebrated hedge veg stalls.

As Guernsey is rich in fish and shellfish, I have included
some seafood dishes and there are also a few dishes
from the Occupation era, when locals had to manage
with very little, and needed to use all their ingenuity to
make food go around.

I hope that this little book will give you a little
'Flavour of Guernsey', and a nice souvenir
of your stay in our lovely Island.

Traditional Recipes

photo: Guerin Collection

History of the Guernsey Bean Jar

Guernsey Bean Jar is a traditional one pot meal, that is wholesome and a perfect winter warmer. This dish was usually prepared at home. Then tied with brown paper, and identified with the family's name. The pot was then taken to the bakers, who would place it in the still hot ovens overnight, where it would cook very slowly.

A family member then collected the bean jar and a small fee was paid to the bakery. Bean Jar recipes vary considerably, as every family had their own specially handed down version.

Traditionally a pig's trotter was the meat basis for this dish, but some recipes use a shin of beef, or belly of pork.
Most people like to eat a bean Jar the day after it has been made, as the flavours have matured.

The Bean Jar itself is a large glazed earthenware pot, with a lid, that is still made & sold in Guernsey.

Recipe for Guernsey Bean Jar

Ingredients

Half a pound of haricot beans
Half a pound of butter beans
1 lb onions – chopped
2 large carrots – diced
1 bay leaf
Salt & pepper to taste
2 pints of beef stock or water.
1 or 2 pig's trotter or a shin of beef
(you could use belly pork as an alternative).

Method

Soak the beans overnight and then drain. Place the beans in a pan, along with the meat, onions and carrots. Pour over the stock or water and bring to the boil. When piping hot, place all ingredients into your casserole or Bean Jar, cover with a lid and place in a pre-heated oven at 150 - 170°C. Cook for 6 to 8 hours, or until the beans are tender. You may need to top up the stock or water as necessary during cooking as the beans will soak up a lot of the juices. The meat should fall of the bone, and these should then be removed before serving.

Taste and adjust seasoning. Serve with warm crusty bread, Guernsey butter, and a glass of Cider.

Guernsey Gâche

This delicious fruit loaf is pronounced Gosh!
It is usually served at teatime and is lovely toasted,
with lashings of Guernsey Butter.

Ingredients

    1 lb plain flour
    ½ lb guernsey butter,
    12 oz sultanas
    1 oz fresh yeast or 1 packet of dried yeast.
    2 oz mixed peel
    1 tsp salt
    1 tsp sugar, pinch salt
    150 ml of milk or warm water.

Method

Sieve together the flour and
the salt, and put the bowl in a
warm place. Cream together
the yeast and the sugar,
adding a little warm water,
until yeast is dissolved then
add the rest of the water and
Leave to stand in a warm
place until it froths. Rub the
fat into the flour, then make a well in the centre, and
add the yeast mix, then add the rest of the water until you
get a stiff dough add the fruit, and Knead lightly. Cover
and leave to prove in a warm place for about 1½ - 2 hours.
Turn the mix into a 1lb loaf tin and bake for 30 minutes
at 200°C. Reduce the heat to 180°C for a further 30
minutes, turn out and cool before serving.

Butter Making, Guernsey.
Guerin, Publisher.

Guernsey milk is amongst
the best in the world

Guernsey Gâche

Ingredients

- 1 lb sultanas or currants
- 1 oz fresh yeast mixed with 1/8 pint of tepid water.
- ½ pint of lukewarm milk or water
- 1 ½ lb plain flour
- ½ lb guernsey butter
- ½ teaspoon of nutmeg
- pinch of salt
- teaspoon of sugar

Method

Use a warm bowl and sift flour with salt. Mix the yeast with sugar and the tepid water, and allow to stand until yeast begins to froth.

Meanwhile, rub the butter into the warmed flour and add the dried fruit, and nutmeg.

Pour in the yeast mixture followed by the rest of the liquid, mix until a dough forms and the mixture comes away clean from the bowl.

Put the dough into a clean basin and cover with a damp cloth, allow to rise for about 1 ½ hours.

When well risen, remove from the bowl and knead a little, place in a well greased loaf tin

And bake in a moderate oven Gas mark 6 or 180°C for an hour.

Allow to cool and serve with Guernsey butter.

Thanks to Rex & Val , the Castel Farmers Market.

Guernsey Gâche Melée

Gâche (pronounced gosh) is the Norman French word for Cake. So Gâche Melée is Apple Cake, however this is rather like a pudding and is usually served with fresh Guernsey Cream, at the end of a meal.

Ingredients

> 1 –2 lbs cooking apples peeled cored and sliced.
> 1 lb plain flour
> 1 tsp cinnamon, 1 tsp grated nutmeg
>   & the grated rind of 1 lemon.
> 8 oz guernsey butter
> 8 oz demerara sugar
> 3 medium eggs

Method

Slice the apples and mix with the sifted flour, grated lemon rind and spices. Mix together thoroughly and leave for a couple of hours to allow apple juices to seep out. Cream together the butter and sugar and add the beaten eggs, a little at a time. Add the egg mixture to the flour mix and stir well until combined. Place the mixture in a greased baking tin, and bake in a moderate oven - 170°C (gas 3) for about 90 minutes or until top has browned. Sprinkle some sugar on top and allow cooling. Serve warm with Guernsey Cream.

Makes 12 portions

Another Guernsey Gâche Melée Recipe

As with all local recipes, there are lots of different versions of these dishes around, many have been handed down for generations.

Ingredients

    1 - 2 lbs of cooking apples (weighed after paring and coring)
    6 oz self-raising flour
    5 oz sugar
    3 fluid oz guernsey milk
    2½ oz suet grated.
    Pinch salt, and a little cinnamon if desired.

Method

Chop the apples into small pieces. Place all the ingredients in a bowl and stir well until thoroughly mixed and apples all coated in the flour. Place this mixture into a well-greased baking pan (7" by 9") and bake for 1½ hours, until golden brown and the apples are cooked.

Cut into squares, and serve with cream or ice cream.

Guernsey Biscuits

These are really bread rolls, not biscuits, which makes the name of them a bit misleading! They are however, a very nice bread roll with a firm crust and nice soft centre.

Ingredients

    1 lb plain flour - sieved
    1 oz fresh yeast, creamed with 1 tsp sugar
    ½ pint of guernsey milk and hot water mixed
    4 oz. guernsey butter
    ½ tsp salt, ½ tsp sugar

Method

Mix some of the liquid with the creamed yeast, and sprinkle with flour. Cover and leave.

Mix together all the dried ingredients, rub in the flour with the butter. Make a well in the middle of the mixture and pour in the yeast mixture to make dough that leaves the sides of the bowl clean. Knead well, cover with a damp cloth, and set aside in a warm place to rise for about 1 hour. Turn out the dough and knead again. Form the mixture into balls and flatten into biscuit shapes. Place the biscuits onto a greased baking tray and leave to prove for 15 minutes. Pre-heat the oven to 200°C (gas 6), then bake the biscuits until lightly browned, (about 30 minutes).

Guernsey Biscuits
are nice to take on a
picnic to the bluebell
woods or to the coast.

Guernsey Buttermilk Cake

This recipe is made with a buttermilk substitute, but can be made with shop purchased buttermilk; you will get the same result. It is very nice at teatime.

Ingredients

- 4 oz sultanas
- 12 oz currants
- 4 oz guernsey butter,
- 1 lb plain flour (sieved)
- 8 oz. demerara sugar
- 3 medium guernsey eggs (whisked)
- 2 oz chopped mixed peel
- 2 level teaspoons baking powder
- 2 level teaspoons bicarbonate of soda
- 1 level teaspoon cream of tartar
- ¼ level teaspoon ground ginger
- 1 level teaspoon grated nutmeg
- ¼ level teaspoon salt
- ½ pint of buttermilk (made by adding 1 tablespoon of vinegar to milk to make ½ pint)

Method

Grease and line a 9" Square, 3" deep Cake Tin. Mix together the dry ingredients. Rub in the butter lightly until the mixture forms breadcrumbs. Stir in the sugar, hollow out centre and add the eggs to the mix, then gradually add the buttermilk. Wash and dry the fruit then stir in with the mixed peel and turn into the prepared tin. Bake in the centre of a pre heated oven at 160°C for 2½ hours or until the top is golden brown.

Traditional Guernsey Cake

Ingredients

    8 oz castor sugar
    4 oz guernsey butter
    5 medium guernsey eggs (separated)
    6 oz self-raising flour

Method

Cream together the butter and sugar, then add the egg yolks one at a time. Beat the flour into the butter mix. Whisk the egg whites until stiff, and then fold in the egg whites until the mixture is an even consistency.

Put the mixture into an 8" buttered baking tin, and bake at 170°C for approx 60 minutes. Turn out and cool before serving.

French Halles & Markets in Guernsey

Until the 1780's, produce was sold in the High Street, A new market was built beneath the new Assembly rooms (now the Guille-Alles Library) in the early 1780's.

Nearly 50 years later fine new meat, fish and fruit markets were constructed in Market Square.

The markets flourished until the early 21st century and the market buildings were in need of repair, the lease was acquired by a developer who undertook the repairs, restored and updated the buildings and rented out retail space, replacing the traditional market.

Many locals have happy memories of shopping in the old markets, particularly at Christmas time, when the poultry were hung around the meat markets and holly and ivy decorated the flower markets.. Christmas Trees were sold outside along the railings of the old French Halles.

The Fish Market was a particular draw for many visitors to the Island, who marvelled at the variety of fish and shellfish on sale, especially the children who were amazed to see live lobster and crabs.

Although we still have a great variety of wonderful fresh available produce, there is no longer a centrally located market in the town, and most modern shopping is now done in the supermarket environment.

The Old Guernsey Markets

Market Square

Fish market

All photos: Guerin Collection

Old French Halles flower
and vegetable market

seafood recipes

photo: Maurice Breh

photo: S

photo: SB

Channel Island Fish & Shellfish

Guernsey & Jersey are famous for the wonderful fresh fish and shellfish found in the waters around their coasts.

Bass, Brill, Mackerel, Monkfish, Red Mullet, Sole, Long Nose and Turbot, being just a few of them. The area is especially rich in shellfish and Guernsey can boast a wonderful variety.

Crab – both Chancre and Spider Crabs, Lobster, Mussels & Scallops are still plentiful.

Spider Crab

Ingredients

　　1 local spider crab, salt & pepper
　　vinegar & very salty water.

Method

Place your live crab in a pan of warm salted water, cover and bring to the boil. Boil briskly for about 15-20 minutes for a 1 - 2lb Crab. Allow to cool. When cold, remove body from shell – discard dead men's fingers (lungs). Remove the body meat, and pick as much meat as possible from the legs & claws. Season to taste, with salt and pepper and vinegar. Serve with bread & butter. Delicious

Ormers

The Ormer is a mollusc, sometimes called an abalone, found off the coasts of the Channel Islands. It is closely related to the Limpet, but has a flattened oval shaped shell. It is usually only exposed at the lowest of the spring tides. There are strict rules about gathering them nowadays as they are in danger of stock depletion. Any Ormer must be at least 8 cm long when collected. They are quite hard to find and locals go out wading in the rock pools in the hope of finding this local delicacy. The dates Ormering is allowed are very specific, in order to protect stocks. The Ormer takes its name from the shape of its mother of pearl shell, and you will see some of the shells decorating the walls in some Island gardens.

Ormers are prepared for cooking by removing from the shell, discarding the entrails and scrubbing off the black slime around the foot. The white firm flesh is then beaten with a rolling pin to tenderize. The traditional method of cooking is in a casserole, although they can be fried. Ormers have a very unique flavour.

Casseroled Ormers

Prepare ormers as previously described.

Roll Ormers lightly in flour, and fry gently in Guernsey butter until slightly brown. Place them in a casserole dish with a slice of bacon, a sprig of parsley, 1 bay leaf, a little chopped onion and salt and pepper to taste. Pour over fish stock, enough to just cover them and bake for 4 hours in a slow oven.

Ormers - Alternative Recipe

Ingredients

2 oz unsalted guernsey butter
1 finely chopped onion
4 oz streaky bacon – chopped
1 clove garlic   1 bouquet garni

12 small ormers – well beaten
Half a pint of dry white wine
Salt & pepper – chopped Parsley
Beurre Marie (1oz Butter
   mixed with 1 oz Flour)

Method

Melt the butter in a frying pan; gently fry the onion and bacon. Add the garlic and ormers. Fry gently for about 10 minutes, then add the wine and seasoning. Add the bouquet garni, cover the pan and simmer for a further 10 minutes. Place the fish on a serving dish. Stir the beurre marie into the liquid until dissolved and thickened. Pour this sauce over the fish and sprinkle with chopped parsley, season to taste, and serve at once with freshly baked Guernsey biscuits.

Fish stock, enough to just cover them and bake for 4 hours in a slow oven.

Fish soup

photo: SB

Ingredients

    4 leeks,
    2 large onions
    2 large carrots
    2 tablespoons olive oil
    2 lb of Tomatoes & 1 tablespoon tomato paste
    6 cloves garlic
    1 bouquet garni
    Parsley, salt & pepper
    8 lbs fresh mixed fish, as available.
    (use cheaper types of fish such as gurnard, whiting and conger)
    cleaned and gutted and leave whole.
    A large glass of dry white wine.

Method

Clean and chop vegetables – sweat down in a very large pan in the olive oil. Chop tomatoes and add to pan, along with crushed garlic. Cook for about 15 minutes. Add the tomato paste and parsley and stir in. Put the fish on top of the vegetables and pour on 8 pints of water to cover the fish, add the wine and bouquet garni. Bring to the boil.

Now liquidize the fish and soup. After all is blended, using a sieve pass the soup a little at a time through the sieve pressing down with a spoon. Discard all bones and flesh that doesn't go through sieve. Return to the pan and cook gently. Serve with croutons and rouille, and sprinkle with some grated Gruyere cheese.

Rouille - goes well with fish soup

This is a sort of chilli, garlic mayonnaise, which is good with cold seafood or mixed into fish soup. Originally a Northern French recipe.

Ingredients

2 small red peppers
5 cloves of garlic
1 small fresh red chilli
A few saffron strands
1 teaspoon salt
1 potato boiled in its skin then peeled and mashed.
200 mls olive oil

Method

Bake the peppers in a pre-heated oven around 200°C until they have browned in places. Remove the skin, and seeds. Place in a mortar or strong bowl and crush with the garlic, chilli, saffron and salt. Once this is all completely mixed together add the mashed boiled potato, gradually adding the olive oil a little at a time, beating well between, until the sauce becomes thick and creamy. Continue until all the oil is used. Taste and adjust the seasoning if needed.

This sauce is also delicious if spread on croutons and dropped into your soup.

seared scallops & bacon.

Ingredients

    3 fresh guernsey scallops - per person (5 for main course)
    Ask the fishmonger to remove the scallops from the shells,
    or open and clean them yourself.
    3 rashers of streaky bacon (5 for main course)
    Salt & pepper
    Bunch rocket
    A little butter and olive oil mixed

Method

Gently melt the oil & butter, being careful not to burn it.

Dry the cleaned Scallops, season and pop them into the oil mix.
Turn up the heat and cook for about ½ a minute on either
side. Remove from the heat and roll in the bacon, pinning with
a cocktail stick.

Return to the pan and cook gently until bacon cooked.

Serve warm with salad or rocket.

photo: SB

Grilled Mackerel

Ingredients

1 medium guernsey mackerel per person, cleaned and gutted.
You can leave the head on if you wish.
1 lemon
Salt & pepper
Olive oil

Method

Dry the fish with kitchen paper, then brush the fish with olive oil and season. Meanwhile heat the grill to very hot.

Put the fish on some tin foil, and place under the grill, and cook for about 4 minutes per side according to the size of the fish. Remove when crispy and cooked through, place on a dish and squeeze lemon juice over.

Lovely served with summer salad or Guernsey new potatoes.

Guernsey Moules Marinieres

Ingredients

    2kg guernsey mussels (for 4 people)
    1 onion
    1 glass dry white wine
    2 tablespoons flour
    Juice of a lemon
    4 cloves of garlic
    1 bunch parsley
    Salt & pepper
    20g Guernsey butter

Method

Clean & remove the beards from the mussels, discard any that are open. Wash thoroughly and place in a saucepan over a gentle heat, for about 2 minutes to check all mussels are open. Reserve the juices.

Place the butter into the pan along with thinly sliced onions and garlic cloves. Once the onion and garlic are golden, sprinkle on the flour to thicken, add the juice, stirring all the time, then add the white wine. Cook for approx 15 minutes on a gentle heat.

Return the mussels to the pan and heat through.

Add Pepper, freshly chopped parsley and squeeze in lemon juice (optional). Also some people might like to add a little crème fraiche.

Excellent served with thinly cut chips.

Guernsey Produce
& Hedge Veg Stalls

photo: SB

Many people attend the weekly farmers markets for fresh, locally grown produce. Whilst others go to their favourite Hedge -Veg stalls.

Guernsey has a profusion of stalls set out along the roadside or at the front of people's gardens.

It is quite common for people to grow their own vegetables in their gardens. The stalls began as a way for people to sell off unwanted vegetables or fruit when they had a glut.

A lot of trust is involved as the fruit and veg is usually placed in priced up bags, and the purchaser is asked to put the money in either a receptacle or sometimes through the letterbox. Even today it is rare for someone to abuse this trust.

It is a real treat to get some potatoes freshly dug, or freshly cut beans. In the summer you can get some wonderful soft fruits, and you can really taste the difference in this produce that is grown so close to home.

There are also a variety of other foods sold on these stalls including homemade jams, & chutney's, some very good local honey, eggs from free-range hens, (kept in peoples gardens), along with the usual vegetables, plants & flowers.

Nowadays some farmers and greenhouse owners have also set up much bigger roadside stalls, along the same lines.

Fresh fish is still caught commercially around the islands by local fishermen and can be purchased at various outlets, including Seafresh in Town, Rocquaine Sea Farms and from Dobo Robert at Perelle.

Tomatoes

As we had a mild climate Guernsey became famous for its grapes in the 19th Century. Many vineries were built during this time, but later, due to competition from the Mediterranean grape growers, the vineries were given over to the cultivation of the tomato. This had become a very popular fruit in English markets and the tomato became the main cash crop.

During the 60's and 70's the Island was covered in large Commercial Greenhouses, and when flying in to the Island, the sun glinted on them, it seemed they were everywhere! The Island was well known for the 'Guernsey Tom'. Eventually cheaper alternatives became available from Europe, which contributed to the demise of the Industry in Guernsey. There was often a glut of tomatoes, especially if they were not perfectly shaped, and the Islanders became adept at creating Tomato recipes to use them up.

Guernsey Tomato Soup

Ingredients

    2 oz guernsey butter
    2 oz bacon, diced
    1 onion
    4 oz diced carrot
    2 oz plain flour
    2 pints chicken stock
    1 lb tomatoes, washed and quartered
    Salt & pepper to taste.
    Guernsey cream (optional)

Method

Melt the butter, and add bacon, onion and carrot – fry gently until lightly browned. Sprinkle in the flour and mix in, cook to a grainy texture. Slowly add stock, stirring continuously, until thickened. Add the tomatoes, and then bring to the boil. Season with salt and pepper to taste. Then simmer for about an hour. During the cooking, skim off excess froth. Allow to cool, and then sieve to remove pips and skin. Taste and adjust seasoning. Before serving, return to pan and reheat gently, the soup can now be served plain, or if preferred, add some Guernsey Cream, just before serving. Also delicious served with crusty bread.

Garlic Tomatoes

Ingredients

    4 large guernsey tomatoes
    3 oz butter
    3 oz white bread crumbs
    1 oz cheddar cheese
    3 cloves of garlic
    1 oz chopped parsley
    Seasoning to taste

Method

Skin the tomatoes by placing them in a bowl and pouring boiling water over them and allow to stand for a couple of minutes. Remove from the water and the skin will peel off easily.

Cut the tomatoes in half and remove seeds if desired, but keep the tomatoes in their halves. Gently melt the butter with the crushed garlic, and add the tomatoes, gently cooking them until soft.

Remove the tomatoes, reserving the butter mixture, and place in an oven proof dish. Add the bread crumbs and chopped parsley to the butter mix and stir until lightly browned. Pour the crumbly mix over the tomatoes, add the cheese and brown under the grill.

Roasted Tomatoes

Ingredients

    12 medium guernsey tomatoes
    2 - 4 cloves chopped garlic (optional)
    4 tbsp of olive oil
    1 tbsp of vinegar
    Salt and pepper
    A bunch of fresh basil
    2 tbsp of balsamic vinegar

Method

Skin and cut the tomatoes into halves, place in an oven proof dish, cut side up. Season, then sprinkle the chopped garlic over the top, followed by the whole fresh basil leaves. Pour over 2 tbsp of olive oil. Pop in the oven at 180° (gas 6) for about 50 minutes. Remove from the oven and allow to rest, you will have quite a lot of juice do not throw this away as it will mingle with the dressing and be delicious!

When ready to serve, plate up , then whisk together the remaining olive oil and balsamic vinegar, add a little freshly ground black pepper and adjust to your taste, pour over the tomatoes and serve with crusty bread.

Tomato Salad

Ingredients

     5 medium guernsey tomatoes
     3 spring onions
     2 cloves of chopped garlic (optional)
     3 tbsp olive oil
     2 tbsp vinegar
     Salt & pepper
     Coriander or parsley (optional)

Method

Thickly slice the tomatoes and place in a dish. Sprinkle over the finely chopped garlic and spring onions. Add the parsley or coriander at this stage if desired.

Mix the olive oil and vinegar with the salt and pepper and adjust to your taste, then pour over the Tomatoes and allow to rest for a couple of minutes for the flavour to infuse.

Serve Chilled!

Photo: Guerin Collection

Tomato Ketchup

Ingredients

6½ lbs very ripe guernsey tomatoes
1 lb 2oz chopped onions
8 garlic cloves
1 large red pepper, deseeded & chopped
7 oz celery, chopped
8 oz golden granulated sugar
8 fl oz cider vinegar

Spice Mix

15 cloves
20 allspice berries
1 tsp celery seeds
Cinnamon stick,
  broken into pieces
1 tbsp salt
1 tsp Black Peppercorns

Method

Place all of the spice mix in a grinder and whiz until reduced to a powder, or grind with a mortar and pestle.

Put the tomatoes, onions, garlic, pepper and celery in a large saucepan. Cover and cook gently for about 15 minutes until all the ingredients are very soft. Pass the mixture through a fine sieve to get a puree

Return the puree to the pan and add the sugar, vinegar and ground spice mix. Simmer for 20 minutes, stirring frequently, until the mixture thickens.

Remove from the heat and pour into hot sterilized jars or bottles.

This recipe makes approx 5lbs and keeps for up to 6 months. Once a jar or bottle is opened, keep refrigerated.

Most of the working
vineries are now overgrown
and falling down

Stuffed Guernsey Tomatoes with Tuna

Ingredients

 1 very large guernsey tomato per person
 A large can of tuna fish
 Mayonnaise
 Salt and pepper
 Fresh parsley
 Chopped chives

Method

Turn the tomatoes upside down and cut 4 or 5 slices ¾ of the way down, being careful not to cut completely through to the base (it must stay joined up).

Mix Tuna fish with the mayonnaise and season.

Spoon the mixture between the prepared slices of the tomato, taking care to keep the shape visually attractive.

Top with chopped chives and parsley.

Guernsey Toms with Guernsey Goats Cheese

Ingredients

    8oz guernsey goats cheese
    Some cucumber
    3-4 guernsey tomatoes

Photo: Sam Peek

Dressing

    3 or 4 tbsp of extra virgin olive oil
    2 tbsp of white wine vinegar
    ½ teaspoon of dry english mustard
    Salt and pepper
    tbsp of chives

Method

Slice the cheese thickly, alternate on a plate with slices of cucumber.

Make a dressing by mixing together all of the above ingredients.

Drizzle the dressing over the tomatoes and snip the chives over the top.

Serve as a side salad or a starter.

Artisan Foods

There has been a resurge of interest in artisan made foods, and some have been awarded prizes. Notably, cheese making is becoming popular, and there is a very good Fort Grey, goats cheese, along with a variety of other excellent cheeses being made in the Island.

A popular locally made drink is Rocquettes Cider, sold widely around the Island and produced using locally grown fruit.

In the late summer sloes and elderberries are collected from the hedgerows to make sloe gin and elderberry wine and in spring the elderflowers can be collected to make elderflower cordial.

Photo: SB

Photo: Sam Peek

Fresh Goats Cheese

Made locally from
Golden Guernsey Goats milk
From Le Douit Beuval Herd
St. Pierre du Bois
By Peter and Mandy Girard

FORT GREY
blue cheese

Sloe Gin

Sloes are still very plentiful around Guernsey hedgerows and cliff paths, and are collected regularly in the autumn to make this delicious sloe gin. This drink is best drunk after at least 3 months maturing, but keeps indefinitely, though it gets stronger!

Ingredients

Collect enough ripe sloes
   to ½ fill a clean wine bottle
1 bottle of gin (any gin will do)
6oz castor sugar
Clean, sterilised wine bottle, with cap
Funnel

Method

Wash and blot dry the fruit thoroughly, (this is not essential). Prick the fruit well using a pin or needle, taking care not to tear the skin. Place the sloes into a clean wine bottle, they should come about a third to half of the way up the bottle. Cover with the sugar and Gin until the bottle is full (you will not use the whole bottle of Gin, so why not make another bottle of Sloe Gin!). Seal with a screw cap or a well fitting cork.

Every day, turn the bottle to mix the ingredients, do this for about 2 weeks. Thereafter leave to stand for at least 3 months, occasionally rocking the bottle gently from side to side. After 3 months you can strain off the liquid from the fruit into a jug, discard the sloes and then re-bottle it.

Keeps indefinitely, if you can resist! Mmmmmmm........

All Photos: SB

The autumn brings
an abundance of fruit
from which to make
jams and jellys.

Homemade Mayonnaise

Delicious with all kinds of seafood's and salads.

Ingredients

    1 guernsey egg yolk – room temperature
    1 tablespoon english mustard
    1 splash of red wine vinegar
    100 mls oil (made from ½ each of sunflower oil and olive oil)
    Salt and pepper

Method

Separate the yoke from the white.

Make sure all ingredients are at room temperature.

Mix the egg yolk with the mustard, vinegar, and seasoning.

Whisk vigorously, then continue whisking and add the oil, in a very slow stream (you can use a food processor). If you do this carefully it will gradually begin to thicken. When all oil is combined it should be a thick custard like consistency.

You can add herbs or lemon to add a delicate flavour.

Alderney Milk Punch

This drink is made every year on the first Sunday in May. Each publican in Alderney makes their own special variation, and offer a free glass of this homemade cocktail to residents and visitors. As you can imagine this is a very popular day out! And everyone makes the most of trying out all the different versions.

Ingredients

    1 Litre of milk
    2 eggs
    Pinch cinnamon
    Pinch nutmeg
    2 oz caster sugar
    100 mls of rum

Method

Whisk the eggs until frothy, and add the rum and sugar. Place the bowl containing this mixture over a pan of boiling water and whisk until mix holds the trail of a whisk. In a separate pan add spices to the milk and bring to the boil. Pour the milk on to the rum and egg mixture and serve immediately

Guernsey Literary & Potato Peel Pie Society

This book written by American authors – Mary Ann Shaffer, and her niece Annie Barrows, has been a huge best seller since it was published in 2008.

Synopsis;

Set in January 1946: Writer Juliet Ashton, receives a letter from a stranger, a founding member of the Guernsey Literary and Potato Peel Pie Society. A remarkable tale follows, told through the medium of letters between the characters, telling of the events in the island of Guernsey during the German occupation. Intrigued Juliet comes to Guernsey to meet the members of the Society and a blossoming romance begins.

The book has captured the hearts of many of those who have read it, and some even make the journey to Guernsey especially to experience the magic of the Island for themselves. I have tried to find an authentic Potato Peel Pie recipe, and although not actually called pies, the following recipes seem to capture the spirit of the recipe in the book's title. Although I have not actually tried them myself! …

Occupation Recipes

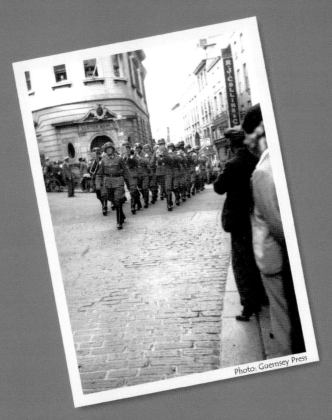

photo: Guernsey Press

During the Occupation of the Channel Islands, food became increasingly scarce. Although many of the residents had evacuated to the Mainland, many locals remained, and of course the Occupying forces boosted the population.

Housewives had to be very creative with the ingredients to hand. Up until 1944 and the arrival of the Red Cross Ship, The Vega, the only food available was either grown or caught in the islands. Meat and dairy products were in very short supply.

Potato Pudding

Ingredients

    1 lb potatoes
    1 Heaped tablespoon sugar
    2 oz dried fruit
    1 egg

Method

Wash, but do not peel the potatoes, grate them and add beaten egg at intervals to prevent discoloration. Add the sugar and dried fruit and mix. Put into an ovenproof dish and bake for about an hour in a hot oven.

Photo: SB

potato peel cake*

Ingredients

Use 3 or 4 potatoes (depending on size)
5 heaped tablespoons of flour
1 heaped tablespoon of sugar
1 level teaspoon baking powder
A pinch of salt
A little Milk, to mix with cinnamon or ginger to taste,
if available, to add flavour.

Method

Clean and peel the potatoes. Boil the peelings until just soft, drain and grate or mash.

Mix together with the flour and sugar and add the baking powder and salt, together with the milk until a soft cake like consistency is achieved. Add flavorings, if available.

Bake in a moderate oven, until lightly browned and cooked through. The unused potato can be used at another meal.

Substituting onions and any available herbs for the sugar can make a savoury version. Season to taste.

Potato scones

Use 1/2 lb dry mashed potato, adding a little salt to taste

Add 1/2 oz of melted margarine and gradually mix in 2 oz of flour.

Combine all these ingredients together and roll out thinly. Cut into squares and prick with a fork. Cook for about 3 minutes on each side on a griddle or in a thick frying pan. Serve hot, with jam.

Potato Pie

Ingredients
- 1 lb potatoes
- 1 onion
- 1/2 cup of milk
- 2 tablespoons of breadcrumbs
- 1/4 oz margarine or Butter
- A little flour
- Salt & pepper

Peel the potatoes thinly and slice them. Place a layer of potatoes in a pie dish followed by a layer of thinly sliced onions and repeat untill pie dish is full. Mix together the flour and seasoning and sprinkle on top of the mixture. Pour over the milk and finish with the breadcrumbs. Dot the butter or margarine over the surface. Bake in a moderate oven for about 2 hours.

Limpet Stew*

Ingredients

A quart of limpets
1 lb peas
1 bay leaf
1 level tablespoon flour
Salt & pepper
Sprig thyme
Chopped parsley
½ pint vegetable or fish stock if available or if not, water.
Small amount of oil

Method

Boil the limpets in their shells for about 10 minutes. Meanwhile boil the peas until cooked. Strain and put aside.

When cooked, remove from the water and take off the shells. Clean away the intestines and finely chop the hard area of the limpet.

Heat oil very gently, with the herbs, then add the flour stirring all the time, add the liquid stock or water to thicken.

Stir in the peas, add soft and chopped limpets, and simmer gently until thoroughly hot. Season and serve with potatoes.

Vegetable Pie*

Ingredients

1 lb mashed potatoes

1 turnip

2 carrots

½ lb haricot beans

½ lb tomatoes

Knob butter

¼ pint of thick gravy

Seasoning

Method

Layer the vegetables and beans alternately in an ovenproof dish and season. Pour over the gravy, and top with mashed potato. Bake in a moderate oven until vegetables are soft when tested, about 30 minutes.

Carrot Marmalade*

Ingredients

2 lbs cleaned & grated carrots

Juice & rind of 4 lemons

3 pints of water

2 lbs Sugar

Method

Boil grated carrots for about an hour. Then add lemon juice and rind then add the sugar and boil again for another hour. Test to see if setting, if not continue to cook a little longer. Allow to cool and jar.

Nb. If you do not have lemons you can add lemon crystals, in their place, but you may need to use some gelatin to set.